CONSIDER
THE
OYSTER

❁

BLANCHE BROWN

NEW MICHIGAN PRESS

TUCSON, ARIZONA

NEW MICHIGAN PRESS
DEPT OF ENGLISH, P. O. BOX 210067
UNIVERSITY OF ARIZONA
TUCSON, AZ 85721-0067

<http://newmichiganpress.com>

Orders and queries to <nmp@thediagram.com>.

ISBN 978-1-934832-76-9. FIRST PRINTING.

Design by Ander Monson.

Cover image by Sylvia Herbold.

CONTENTS

Consider the Oyster   1

Works Cited   45

Acknowledgments   53

oyster from old French *oistre* from Latin *ostrea*

the feminine form of *ostreum* the latinisation

of Greek's ὄστρεον *ostreon* "oyster" one

letter away from *osteon* "bone." known to

the Romans as *calliblepharis* meaning "beautiful eyelids."

pronounced "oyshter" and "oy-ster" and "er-ster" and

"oyscher" "O-EE-stahs" and "OY-stuh" and "eye-sters"

"OY-stah" and "Ur-ster" "arsters" and "Oyshture"

"aw-stuh" "awhsters" the y a mystic appearance.

oh stir. the vowel music followed by consonant

collapse. o sir. spitfull local, the teeth come

together in the middle, syllabic break. all

in the front of mouth, I open with a little oh.

O feast O form eroded : a seaside cave
at Pinnacle Point in South Africa contains
evidence of a shellfish dinner enjoyed by
early humans. the oyster remains date back
165,000 years. the oyster itself evolved about
200 million years ago as one of the first
bivalves to halve in primordial seas.

consider the oyster's
sleep never sleep
on beds of every bottom
sediment sentiment
murk rock root pier
pole sunk ship anchor
consider how they
propel populate keep
peace engine permeable

oysters begin boneless & free floating
    light squirms without burden of back
        larvae fold themselves around
            their few molecules of calcium
                carbonate to layer grow their home bone
                    sifting more calcium out of sea to shell further.
                        the sharpest memories form not from the mundane
                            but the distinctive edge of the new. my first oyster
                                is lost somewhere among shrimp & boiled peanuts
                                    smoked mullet & early baptismal gulf dips. mouthfuls
                                      of warm saltwater. the hour long drive from inland
                                        panhandle swamp to coastal sand an easy one.
                                        the initial gulp I forget, but my first
                                        successful self-served shuck
                                        stays firm

O farm O slow grow O factory music :
Sergius Orata bred oysters on the roof
of his house; caught tide and devised seas.
would place his Roman ear to the unbroken
surface of the sulfur bath water, listen for gurgling.

consider the oyster
clung to twig in
a copper tub. a few
cousins for company
against the metal
some man's hands
tapping the oyster's
roof head. a hose of
bubble troubling
a spat's grip. the great
surplus of algae
clumping along the
bath's rounded edges.

an oyster is a combination of rumor
　　　and change over time. as a child, I climbed
　　　　　shell mountains and chalk rose like steam
　　　　　　　around my white calves. a truckload dump
　　　　　　　　　of thousands split and emptied rushed the ear.
　　　　　　　men with blue rubber-gloved hands barred me
　　　　　　from the buckets full of husks. I learned
　　　　　to stay away from men working. daddy
　　　　　　pulled me aside, showed me how to hold
　　　　　　　the knife, pry the animal open at the hinge.
　　　　　　　　　mud shards flaked at my stabs. knife tucked
　　　　　　　　　　　into joint crevice & wrist wrecking the angle
　　　　　　　　　　　to break the hold and sever the abductor
　　　　　　　　　　muscle. the twist takes time to tackle
　　　　　　　　　　it took me twenty minutes of
　　　　　　　　　　clumsy jabbing at this
　　　　　　　　　　craggy father
　　　　　　　　　　food.

O slow fester O station of the reef:
a waterways liver and indicator
species, chemical compounds from
pharmaceuticals are found in oysters
near water treatment plant outfall pipes.
plant as in : organism of the vegetable
Kingdom, building or machinery used
in manufacturing, decoy or subterfuge
placed strategically to confuse. an oyster
touches and thinks stay. surfactants,
used in detergents, paints, etc at both
the industrial & household level, drain
off and disperse. oysters everywhere
contain them. increased carbon dioxide
levels acidify the sea and reduce calcium
carbonate ions, harming shell development.

consider the oyster
whose abductor is
obliquely striated.
quick translucence
ribbon fibers that tie
shells. together thick
myofilament and
fusiform cells make
a dense body.

a slip and I met the meat of my
own plump. red leaking out to
rivulet dye the living oval. juice
spilled onto ground instead
of into throat. a cut proves
the barrier. the only woman
I remember really shucking was
my biker aunt Reesha. sure-handed
she would also point knotted knuckle
to color. see. shy shades of pink ridge
the sides. a streak of green pulses
the gills. detach the foot and
a black blue spot appears on
the shell which I realize now
is not separate, lifeless, but
an organ of the
organism.

O creature O knife season O weather permitting : people
fear oysters, opening up to what grows beyond sight.
"food becomes abject only if it is a border between
…nature and culture, between the human and nonhuman."
the threat of sick. the sea. a bad oyster will look it. cold
ripples whudder over skin. the result of stale putrefaction.
a bad oyster smells of copper and egg gas and could occur
at any time of the year. the *only eat oysters during months*
with an R in them doctrine has circulated since Samuel Butler's
1599 treatise *Dyet's Dry Dinner*. warm brackish waters encourage
Vibrio vulnificus a bacteria that can be deadly flesh dissolving
for people with compromised immune systems. around fifteen
U.S. cases annually. not a bad oyster but a traceless bacteria.
or an oyster summer's open door. poison walks in. the FDA
issues warnings, menus asterisk raw eat at your own risk. But
all legal measures have met firm cross-party southern opposition.
gulf coast oysters must be pasteurized in California.

consider an oyster's
shell grown one tissue
paper layer at a time. bone
thin into molten. whose
final shape is so mutant
geometry's language
misplaces. a muddy bottom
produces a slender sparse
shell valve. estuary blotches
right valve yellow and purple.
there is never new water
on the back of this world.

when does the swallowed
    raw oyster quit twitching
        its two pairs of nerve cords?
            does the open air do the drowning
                or the acid slosh enzyme bath
                    of belly? down to dead by
                        the time the iron is yanked
                            out of the oyster molecules
                                and flung into protein boats to
                                    traverse my internal absorption
                                        streams. transferrin binds to iron
                                            and transports it to all tissues. I may
                                                have some oyster in my flexor carpi
                                                    ulnaris, in my cranial nerves, in my
                                                        epithelial layers, in my
                                                            uterine lining in my

O seduction O source O hormonal
stew : mollusks are rich in iron zinc
calcium and selenium. vitamins A
and B. gelatinous buttery dollop,
oysters also contain amino acids
that trigger an increase in testosterone
and progesterone hormones. scientists
offer these facts as explanation for
the animal's ancient aphrodisiac
reputation, Casanova opening his
gullet to slick with fifty every morning.
the human study of oyster larvae
is entering its fourth century.
an uncooked oyster is not raw but
living while taken inside. an oyster
supper quivers animal to animal.

consider the oyster
building up fat and
color density the steady
doubling down upon
their own guts packing
themselves with copies
of themselves

flat oysters fertilize within the shell but
the eastern oyster dominates the market and secretes
eggs and spews sperm projectile into tide. spawning
when waters reach 68 degrees. milt let loose & milk clouds
collide. spat are free swimming for two weeks and then cement
themselves onto the first clean hard object found. left foot
permanently bound. I've seen clusters stud a plastic buoy
a barrier I made a game of crossing. prodantric, oysters
spend the first years of life as males then transition into
egg production which requires more energy, maturity.
all his crinkly fringes surge to mother. self-fertilization
seems but isn't possible. an oyster glides between
genders like how a salty beach spot tastes
swampy after a flood and in
the throes of discharge
turns translucent.

O flavor O fondle frond
O primer palate :
if you like the taste
of oysters then
you'll like taste
just like
looks like
smells like

an oyster

is only an
aphrodisiac if you
think it is. musk
mucus of neck crook.

consider the oyster
sift taste of algae
green breath how
keen and calm
the oyster licks
up plankton. a brine
brews in and on
the oyster. salt
circling. milksweet.

an oyster on
the tongue is not
unlike a tongue
on the tongue wet
form against wet form
the difference lies in
temperature. never eat
a warm raw oyster. a sour
that will stick and turn in
gut until refusal is the only
response to marshsalt
smell of seafood on
the table. what enters
the oyster enters
me coolly.

O swallow O mouthful O mineral merrior :
oyster flavors hold their habitat. vegetal algae
notes, salinity pricks, river mud grass, limestone
mineral metals sharp. sweet cream smooth from heat,
rock lick, the copper rust that comes from acid,
melon, cold deep water creates a spring green flavor.
slow growth in nutrient-rich water builds plump.
oysters place taste, put their home in your mouth.
an oyster dunks its predator in its waters. the mouth
is a portal. an oyster is one large mouth. oysters thrive
in the mouths of bays. a couple of species have sprung
into hundreds of brand names. copyright mouths
cultivated to a timed tang and served. gnarled wild
oysters rarely reastauranted anymore, the gulf coast is one
of the few places where wild oysters are still harvested.

consider the oyster
nestled against kin
immobile as the starfish
encircles and plies
apart its halves, thrusts
stomach onto into its
still prey. how the oyster
wanes. thin cracker
shells under the boring
sponge. the weight
of other mollusks,
younger oysters.

oysters are bivalve mollusks. they can be true, wellfleet,
bluepoints, thorny, Chincoteague, pilgrim, saddle, Lynnhaven,
kumamoto, moonstone, mystic, Permaquid, Island Creek and
windowpane. I can always distinguish an Apalachicola from a Calabash.
a heavy soft hand full of salt versus a thimble. in the 1800s, Apalachicola
was the third largest port in the gulf and shipped barrels of oysters
on steamers. until 2013, Apalach was still known as one of the best
oystering tributaries in the country. protected by small barrier islands,
the calm bay marks where the Apalachicola River, a thick brown
sluggish trail that drains southern Georgia and the Florida
highlands, gulfs out. lined by cypress and tupelo
swamps, the river's tannin tinted water is rich and
filled with sediment, oyster feed.

O catch O cull O shell bleached white : 90% of Florida's
oyster haul comes from Apalachicola Bay where oysters are
neither dredged nor grown in sacks but harvested like they
were in 1836 with wooden-handled scissor-shaped fourteen-
foot tongs. oystermen pull oysters straight from the beds into
their small wide boats. when the shallow bay was healthy
it supported about 300 oystermen who bagged the oysters
by hand and sold them directly to restaurants along the working
waterfront. in 2012 a dozen cost ten dollars. or the bags arrived
at processors and seafood markets. bushels bulging with fresh
mud-in-cranny oysters often twinned onto each other. regional
bars and restaurants boasted "fresh from Apalach" whose
low-lying reefs carry names: North Spur, West Lump, Paradise,
Bayou Flats, Mast Pole, Picaleen, Cat Point, Haggens Flat,
Porters Bar, Dry Bar, East Hole, Cabbage Top

consider the oyster
in a semi-truck crossing
freeways consider
the absence of time tide
sun and waiting for salt
water in a cardboard box
or styrofoam packed in
almost like a reef but
without a foothold

what began as a taste
        craved accumulated into
            a love for all the oyster
                could signify. I took
                    my body to the needle.
                        the desire to display
                            an oyster image did
                                not prevent me from
                                    folding when the bro tattooist
                                        turned and said *but it looks like*
                                            a vagina, I'm gonna draw
                                                the shells empty and I
                                                    consented *yeah, right, okay* as
                                                        if that was not an obvious simile.
                                                            and now strangers ask me
                                                                is that an avocado
                                                                    on your arm

O slice O glove O morning hours O stiff forearms O wet underfoot:
a 1919 report from the Children's Bureau of the U.S. Labor Department
on the working conditions in oyster canneries along the gulf coast,
examined nine communities from Louisiana, Mississippi, and
Florida. men brought in the catch. women and children shucked
for the canneries. 65% of the children worked the regular irregular
factory hours. dark wet dawn. wooden slats, metal pails to catch
the freed meat. pictures show them standing next to shell piles
high as their necks with knives blurring. a younger child a smear of
white fabric running. "of the 1,350 children included in the study,
only 9 were foreign born; 473 were Negro; and the rest, 868,
were native white." *native white* is an oxymoron. all children earned
less than the women. everyone was paid by pound shucked & rates
varied from 1.5 cents to 5 cents. this was before the 1938 Fair Labor Standards Act.
in 2016, Crystal Seas Seafood in Pass Christian, Mississippi relies on HB-2 sanctioned
seasonal workers, primarily men from Mexico. Crystal Seas pays
its shuckers $9.65 an hour and advertises "succulent reef fresh flavor."
the national average hourly rate for shucking was $11 an hour at the time.
workers sit at metal stations and use hammers to speed up the shucking process.

consider how the oyster makes
a pet of being kept. seduces humans
into protecting reefs from predators.
into ensuring breeding keeps its
smack. into measuring temperatures
and providing spats with tiles,
bamboo shoots, docks, netting.

an oyster serving, for human feeding, is six medium
sized specimens and contains four grams of protein and
about 200% of the recommended daily B-12 intake.
an otter might make the meal matter more. jagged
and closed, an oyster is private even among other
oysters. half hung open and interior exposed,
an oyster is public even among other mollusks.
oysters lump and pop and wait in splendid passivity
for a feast of flecks: plankton, bacteria, organic matter,
detritus. an oyster's three-chambered heart pumps
steady and colorless, smaller than my pinky nail.
exhalent chamber opposite inhalent chamber.

O been O has O be O is :
An oyster has often been the food of the poor
An oyster has often been a delicacy for the rich
An oyster has often been a street food shucked
from wooden stalls or carts
An oyster has often been paired with wines and beers
An oyster has often been called a 19th century animal
An oyster has often been the first course in a feast
fettered upon silver platters
An oyster has often been doused in vinaigrette
An oyster has often been a symbol of gluttony
An oyster has often been smeared with cocktail sauce
a mixture consisting of mainly horseradish and ketchup
An oyster has often been slurped in taverns
An oyster has often been misread
An oyster has often fluctuated in cost and fashion
An oyster has often been a hearty winter meal
An oyster has often been squirted with fresh lemon
An oyster has often been made a moralizing morsel

consider the oyster
the clack their dead
make. the three hundred
strong filter gurgle that
must treble the water
of a healthy reef. even
alive the animal appears
lifeless. reed song speech.
consider the urgency
of milt and how muscles
learn to feel shadows.

an early oyster remembers
    St. George Island, a short drive from
        Apalach. I'm a May worm in the brownblue
            water. too young to understand anything except
                my parents are loud angry. mommy seeks retreat
                    and races me on a back road. black rock rises
                        up to meet her. her face broken loose by drink
                          and or. the loss of measure. then her knee too
                            is red. daddy still a scream behind us. we end up
                          at an oyster bar on the beach. mommy kept me
                              a lap pet all night near, something to knee bounce.
                                to protect or use as protection. the oysters felt too
                                slimy but I slurped to please. the empty
                            shells swam, floated like abandoned
                        canoe hulls in their
                          melted ice bed.

O host O foundry O stretch of open
bone : any brine or brack makes an
intertidal or subtidal water hospitable
to oysters which form their own reefs
soldering onto one another. a keystone
species, oysters provide habitats for :
mussels, barnacles, anemones, anchovies,
blue crab, Croaker, flounder, herring,
shrimp, spanish mackerel, numerous sponge
species, silver perch, flatworms, rocksnails,
gobies, drum, snappers, the jingle shell, conchs, etc.

consider the oyster
spent from spewing
itself. the oyster drained
of matter and color
becomes a thin mucous
spread inside its shell
after the hot exertions
in august waters.

on April 20, 2010, the *Deepwater Horizon* offshore
    drilling rig exploded pouring millions of gallons of crude
        oil into the Gulf. some stopper unstopped sopped. I was
            a junior in high school. I hadn't kissed a girl since I was ten.
                vulnerable coast economies. In 2012, Governor Scott declared
                    a "Commercial Fishing Resource Disaster" in Apalachicola Bay.
                      in 2015, BP paid 1 million to the City of Apalachicola for lost revenue.
                          but oil never entered the bay or washed ashore. unlike Louisiana thick
                            with it. the lawsuit laid on the slick grounds of business loss due
                              to perception. water is a system. lucky the gulf moves wholly.
                                during spill, the state ordered an emergency full harvest.
                                stripped reefs. another layer of stress slathered.
                              on top of steadily increasing low-flow
                              periods, low catch, etc.

O border O bother O brother O breath:
before during and after the spill, Georgia sucked
up fresh water to hydrate Atlanta and its company
of suburbs. a running sink. the panhandle churned
saltier and saltier. less brackish conditions opened
the bay to more oyster predators and less
phytoplankton. Apalach oystermen started
returning with one sack instead of twenty. stores
emptied. Florida, Georgia and Alabama have wrangled
for 30 years over water. how much by who for what
and why the future uses. the Tri-State Water War.
repeated court battles, congressional power plays,
& a brief bid to move state lines. all three lay claim
to the water flowing through the interconnected
Apalachicola-Chattahoochee-Flint river basin.

consider the oyster
at low tide. sun lapping
at its layers. grasses
bristle. a water swallow
held tight by valves
keeps the animal slick
as air brushes. or if
a shallow wash remains
the warm water runs
through and the open
oyster's gray-white oval
flesh can be bird spotted.

oysters do not allow
for ambivalence. it is pray
or prey, pry or pursed.
the human animal either
seeks to suck or shuns.
of the shellfish, oysters
are the grittiest. a hasty
shuck leaves behind sand,
shell bits, hard points
in an otherwise glide
glug of slime. the dive bars
daddy took me to were
often covered in dollar bills,
confederate flags, Harley Davidson
paraphernalia. I felt at home.
shame is hot when
I enter now.

O battleground O drinking well O own O marketplace :
federal law mandates river flow. each state solid liquid
gas owns the right to an equal water share. the Apalachicola-
Chattahoochee-Flint basin flows from northeast Georgia south
through Atlanta along the Alabama border and empties into
Florida. a dam can create a tragedy of the commons.
the commons have been damned. in 1956, the Army
Corps of Engineers completed the Buford Dam resulting
in Lake Lanier named for poet and confederate Sidney
Lanier. the lake was meant to level the supply and provide
a water bank for all three states, flood control,
hydropower, to circumvent the cycles of drought and
flood common to the southeast. but, Atlanta boomed
and the Corps began issuing water supply contracts without
authorization, without the evaluation required by the National
Environmental Policy Act, without monitoring Georgia's
withdrawals, without considering how a dam blocks the flow
of fresh water over an Apalach oyster's open face.

consider the oyster
minutely gilling
consider how oyster
shells are used to
restore oyster reefs
consider the tremor
of reef break and
the slow restoration

an oyster is a tissue
swirl four folds of
delicate external gills
frill lip. under these
lie the labial palps,
soft flaps that sort
consumption between
which the inverted
u-shaped mouth
slit fits. I supplicant.
I lip prey to shell.
to dip carcass back
I must bow to
oyster, risk dribble,
baby a little

O tip O tendril O timbre of throat salt :
"Tipping the Velvet" like how tonging easily
becomes tonguing is a Victorian euphemism for
cunnilingus. In Sarah Waters's novel of the same
name, the oyster-loving lesbian protagonist claims
"I have never doubted my own oysterish sympathies
…catch the scent of liquor and brine beneath my
thumb-nail and in the creases of my palm." The opening
credits of BBC's adaptation piles the oysters
on thick, open and shoreline a-tumble.

consider the oyster.
how spat attempt
to stick together. a
body of many. larvae
look to land on
populated reefs. in
disregard of risk, for
adult oysters eat spat.
a slip into mouth.
yet, oysters seek
other oysters.

I once dreamed an oyster grew, spiked and
     swirling, large enough to gulp dozens of me. inside
          the crooked countenance I held hands with three
               of my brood. it was cool slippery within the porcelain
                    interior. *Florida v Georgia* is just one of the many court
                         cases connected to the water wars connected to the oyster
                              crop failure in Apalach. since 2014, Florida has spent $57 million
                                   in tax dollars litigating water. in June 2018, the US Supreme Court
                                   remanded the case back to special master, meaning make
                                        your case again. it is not clear if capping water usage in Georgia
                                        would even solve the Apalachicola basin's health crisis.
                                        viable. soluble. solute. via. life. water. duct. what
                                        long term. forge what way forward. for
                                        the river system overall. a moon
                                        descendant, the oyster waxes
                                        wanes with water
                                        health.

O night beach O evening tide:
Salvianus wrote in "De Piscium
natura et Preperatione" that if much
partaken of, oysters will dispose one
to melancholy and to the feeling,
in one's sleep, of phantoms and incubi.

consider the oyster
how grit enters its
held open body
and is passed over
let loose allowed
through. the mollusks
that produce pearls
belong to a different
scientific family.
Aviculidae instead
of Ostreidae. but one
shell against another
shell is still solid anchor.

our front porch rails cultivated
oyster husks hard bone studs
but only the special ones:
doubles or triples backsides
seared together, giants, tinies,
any shell with a strong luster
glowing pink or black or
incandescent, a row lined
the wood and baked in
the sun. and those shells
that did not become display
were nestled into garden
beds whole or ground up. oyster
shells regulate pH levels, increase
fertilizer uptake, enhance soil
tilth, and improve
compost

O spuds O spoil: five years after
the deepwater horizon disaster,
the national wildlife federation
reassessed the damage. despite
broad long term estuary decline,
in 2010 the gulf still produced
two-thirds of the nation's oyster
harvest. the spill exposed the eastern
oyster to oil and its dispersants.
PAHs can be lethal to oyster
gametes, embryos, larvae, juveniles
and adults. their sub-lethal effects
include: reduced reproductive success
as in jet of milt and spat to rock.
oysters are unable to move away
from soiled areas. estuaries like
Pensacola Bay & Mississippi Sound
have each lost more than 90% of
their historical oyster reefs

consider how in death
the oyster generates.
returns nutrients,
even to the inland
garden. how in death
it builds the ocean floor
becomes rock sediment
earth ground food

low tide bouquets, oysters often muck
aggregate along riverside. pluff mud in
estuaries makes oyster clumps the only
safe footpath through the sulphur brack's
avenging suck. for oysters settle on other
oysters, heavenward spirals as wild as.
clusters must be broken into shuckable
single bellies in the palm. an oysterperson's
culling hammer measures size as it severs
bonded backs. oyster clumps like concrete.
there is a shrimp boat in Apalach named
Miss Martha. Martha is my mother's name.
one year she glued oyster shells into wreaths
and I made oyster angel wings that
hung crooked from
red ribbon.

O Fancy: the Dutch Masters included
oysters in both genre and still life paintings.
it was often the main or only food depicted
as being eaten. taken. genre painters put
the oyster in two contexts: the merry making
feast and the cornered tryst. in Dirk Hals's
Party of Young Men and Women at Table, 1625
oyster shells skirt the floor like a crumb trail.
in Frans van Mieris's *Oyster Meal* 1661 a
dewy woman holds a thin oyster between
her thumb and forefinger a glass slipping out
of her hand a man leaning over. in Gabriel Metsu's
Oyster Meal, 1661-1667, a woman picks up
an oyster from the plate being tilted towards
her by the man leaning over her seated frame.
she aims her oyster fork at flesh. in Jan Steen's
Oyster Girl, 1665, a girl holds an oyster up a small
smile before eating and stares at the viewer the white
of her eyes matching the gleam of the shell's interior.
the viewer the man peering over. Jan Steen
A man offering an oyster to a woman 1665

consider the little filter oyster
mouth that opens only a little
but allows whole oceans to pass
within. consider how oil may miss
the oyster only for the dispersant
Corexit® 9500 to slip in. consider
the oyster's immune system for
which the dispersant is more toxic
than oil. consider cascade. tide wind.

even after the divorce, daddy still sent
    gifts. once a framed two-feet wide
        photograph of the Miss Martha was left
            propped on the back patio of mom's new house.
                a surprise seeps. Martha's hull a slim step into
                    the water. mom put it up. mom took it down.
                        it hung briefly in the kitchen like a hole in the eye.
                          an insecticide tickling throat. in 1969, DDT was found
                            in 99 % of oyster samples taken from Mobile Bay. another
                              gulf coast oyster capital. DDT levels spiked in late winter
                          and early spring during max freshwater inflows. pesticide
                        levels in oysters coincide with levels found in
                          composite samples of 12 major food groups
                          comprising the American food
                          supply and are not considered
                        significant.

O law O land O bounty of bonded feet : in 1959
a poacher named Berkley Muse was killed in smoke
curling over water. gunfire from an oyster patrol boat
on the Potomac River. during an outbreak of territorial
oyster wars. when water was wild. Muse dredging
the night. police claim the boat gave chase. it was not
the first time Maryland Oyster Police bullets had struck
buildings in town. the death prompted President Kennedy's
1962 Potomac River Fisheries Commission. which outlines
permissions and proper properties and lines and guides and
catch limits and licenses. plant protein carefully. fish out chaos.

an oyster disrupts and
thrives in the disturbance
of fresh and salt running
into each other the shift
of motion as ocean reaches
shallow mud and sand
kicked up the shoreline
a chaotic border not quite
a fish a rooted animal

a secret slides an oyster leaves a trail

my mouth works to follow out down into

earth elements ions. almost five decades

before Florida filed the current suit seeking

to reallocate water in the basin, residents complained

pollution from upstream Georgia was harming

the Apalachicola River. less than 1/4 of 1% of U.S.

rivers are protected as National Wild & Scenic Rivers

that is about 3,000 miles out of 3 million. segments

of recreational richness. of the 12 current campaigns

to add protections, Virginia is the only southern state.

I drink the oyster that drains the run-off of its heavy

metals. state's rights are always code for

getting away with. *American Rivers*

labeled the Apalachicola

River endangered

in 2016.

O paint O pint O silver pitcher pitching forward :
white flesh tones cupped in mother of pearl
shimmer surrounded by rough ruffles Dutch
still-leven like a still heaven. haven. level life.
hold the common close. look into the face of
an oyster. an oyster is a looking glass. a glint
of light. Osias Beert's *Bodegon* bejeweled
the oyster in dobs of glossy oil afloat in their
own lifeblood. later *Banquet Piece with Oysters
Fruit and Wine* upturned ovals in echo. Wilhelm
Heda put the viewer's nose to what they nose
Still-Life with Oysters Rum Glass and Cup.
naked oyster body bare in the northern air
a puddle in its own silver. oyster liquor &
nacre multiples surface glow. Jan de Heem
Still Life with A Glass and Oysters

consider the oyster
that isn't planted
to be eaten. the ones
who filter 50 gallons
a day of industry
and sewage. whose
waters are past
poison. the mature
suckers who gulp
and strain and do
the work of living.

biomineralization is the capacity
          for self repair. scientists study
                    nacre or mother-of-pearl in vivo
                         bone graft tests. some bonds
                              are perfect. not only can
                                   nacre be grafted and accepted
                                        onto human bone it also releases
                                        active agents which induce bone
                                        regeneration. replace my body
                                        with oyster secretions. filter me out
                                   of me. I never learned how to
                              brake on skates and fractured
                              my ankle. in a navy cast for three
                                   months, a slow heavy humid florida
                                   summer with no swim break.

O cold blooded O current O abundance
O engendered danger: the Apalachicola River
basin contains the highest diversity of amphibians
and reptiles in the United States and Canada. more
than 40 species of amphibians, more than 80 species
of reptiles, more than 1,300 species of plants. more than
a hundred of these are known by humans to be threatened
or endangered. the eastern oyster is not on a watch list.
to be on a list is to be past a point. Georgia, the upstream
user, wants enough water to not worry about supply.
Alabama, downstream, wants water for power, fisheries,
current and future use. Florida, downstream and under,
wants fresh-water to reach Apalachicola Bay. wants to
sustain a multi-million dollar shellfish industry under duress
from low flow, salt. water wants to move to enter oyster.
or oyster wants to open to water.

consider the oyster
clamped against
the waves whipped
up by hurricane force
winds. rattle against
cage or reef. floodwater
flattening river banks
and rushing sediment
out. consider coming
loose in your own body
storm torn and rent.

in August 2018, Cholla Petroleum submitted

    applications for six exploratory wells. the sites,

        if approved, would bore into the 100-year floodplain

            between the Apalachicola River, Chipola River and the Dead

                Lakes in Calhoun County (named for John C. Calhoun a statesman

                    famous for his defense of slavery). Cholla Petroleum proposes to drill

                        12,900 feet down, punching through Florida's aquifer, the state's source

                          of drinking water. daddy's well pumps water to the house from

                            the underground canyons of freshwater gurgling beneath the gun

                              state. I taste stone moss. both surface and groundwater serve

                                as feeders into Apalachicola Bay and the Gulf of Mexico.

                                  the limestone rock that makes up the aquifer's

                                cavernous walls is made of calcium

                                carbonate, like an oyster shell

O sand O bed O channel O reef :
archaeologists make dead oysters talk.
who was opened by fire and who by
sharpened instrument. shells are not
simply masses of calcium carbonate
but are crystals embedded in a conchlion
matrix. the shell deposits and dissolves.
and the oyster like the tree forms fine
bands of growth. periods of stress such as
spawning, severe storms, or excessive
temperatures create a grain. in the southern
oyster the heat shock and spawning break
are often superimposed. the same line.
stained valves speak the weather.

consider the flexible
inflexible body of
the oyster. consider
the tiny cilia curls
at constant calculation.
a gape clean. ripple
rush of wave between
pulp muscle and fine
stone smooth bone.
consider the oyster
does not consider you.

WORKS CITED

Apalachicolariverkeeper.org, apalachicolariverkeeper.org/.

"As State 'Water Wars' Get Salty, Oysters Get a Say." *The Pew Charitable Trusts*, www.pewtrusts.org/en/research-and-analysis/blogs/stateline/2018/07/03/as-state-water-wars-get-salty-oysters-get-a-say.

BlueCircle of Blue. "Infographic: The Oyster Industry in Florida's Apalachicola Bay." *Circle of Blue*, Kayla Ritter. https://www.circleofblue.org/Wp-Content/Uploads/2018/06/Circle-of-Blue-Water-Speaks-600x139.Png, 10 Mar. 2016, www.circleofblue.org/2012/world/infographic-the-oyster-industry-in-floridas-apalachicola-bay/.

Bolitho, Hector. *The Glorious Oyster*. London, Alfred A. Knopf, 1929.

Bryan, William D., and Christopher J. Manganiello. "There's a Solution to the Southeast's Water Crisis. But Will Georgia and Florida Agree to It?" *The Washington Post*, WP Company, 8 Mar. 2018, www.washingtonpost.com/news/made-by-history/wp/2018/03/08/theres-a-solution-to-the-southeasts-water-crisis-but-will-georgia-and-florida-agree-to-it/?utm_term=.277974786f96.

Casper, V. L. *Study of Chlorinated Pesticides in Oysters and Estuarine Environment of the Mobile Bay* Area. U.S. Department of Health, Education, and Welfare, 1969.

"Deepwater Horizon—BP Gulf of Mexico Oil Spill." *EPA*, Environmental Protection Agency, 19 Apr. 2017, www.epa.gov/enforcement/deepwater-horizon-bp-gulf-mexico-oil-spill.

Durrenberger, E P. *It's All Politics: South Alabama's Seafood Industry*. Urbana: University of Illinois Press, 1992.

Effective Monitoring to Evaluate Ecological Restoration in the Gulf of Mexico. The National Academies Press, 2017.

Elliott, Debbie. "7 Years After BP Oil Spill, Oyster Farming Takes Hold In South." *NPR*, NPR, 10 June 2017, www.npr.org/sections/thesalt/2017/06/10/532102196/7-years-after-bp-oil-spill-oyster-farming-takes-hold-in-south.

"Energy Development & Rivers." *American Rivers*, www.americanrivers.org/threats-solutions/energy-development/.

Entriken, Allison. "Turning Tides in Apalachicola." Atlanta Magazine, 7 Feb. 2019, www.atlantamagazine.com/southbound-articles/turning-tides-in-apalachicola/.

Evans, Amy C. "The Oysterman." *THE BITTER SOUTHERNER*, THE BITTER SOUTHERNER, bittersoutherner.com/the-oysterman#.XIcvvxNKjVo.

"The Fight for Water and Oysters (Gravy Ep. 3)." *Southern Foodways Alliance*, 4 May 2015, www.southernfoodways.org/gravy/the-fight-for-water-and-oysters-gravy-ep-3/.

Fisher, M. F. K. *Consider the Oyster*. North Point Press, 1954.

Fixes, Ryan, et al. *Five Years and Counting : Gulf Wildlife in the Aftermath of the Deepwater Horizon Disaster*. NWF, 2015, www.nwf.org/~/media/PDFs/water/2015/Gulf-Wildlife-In-the-Aftermath-of-the-Deepwater-Horizon-Disaster_Five-Years-and-Counting.pdf.

Fuhrmeister, Chris. "The Disappearing Apalachicola Oyster: Florida's Fight to Save Its Prized Delicacy." *Eater*, Eater, 23 July 2015, www.eater.com/2015/7/23/9010545/oysters-apalachicola-bay-florida-georgia-atlanta.

Gerard, James W. *Ostrea; or, The loves of the oysters. A lay. New York,* T. J. Crowen, 1857.

"Gulf Coast Oysters." *Oysterater,* www.oysterater.com/region/gulf-coast/.

"Gulf Coast Oysters Unsafe (But Not For the Reason You Think)." *Trans Fat | Center for Science in the Public Interest,* cspinet.org/new/201006241.html.

"Gulf Oil Spill." *Ocean Portal | Smithsonian,* Smithsonian's National Museum of Natural History, 28 Feb. 2019, ocean.si.edu/conservation/pollution/gulf-oil-spill.

"Half Shell 101." *In A Half Shell,* www.inahalfshell.com/half-shell-101/.

Holton, Jennifer. "The Raw Truth: What's behind Apalachicola's Oyster Problem?" *Content,* www.wjhg.com/content/news/The-Raw-Truth-Whats-behind-Apalachicolas-oyster-problem-472830973.html.

Iijima, Brenda. *Remembering Animals.* Nightboat Books, 2016.

Jacobsen, Rowan. *American Terroir: Savoring the Flavors of Our Woods, Waters, and Fields.* Bloomsbury Press, 2013.

Jacobsen, Rowan. "Apalachicola Bay Notebook" *The Oyster Guide RSS,* www.oysterguide.com/new-discoveries/apalachicola-bay/.

Jacobsen, Rowan. *A Geography of Oysters: the Connoisseurs Guide to Oyster Eating in America.* Bloomsbury, 2008.

Lusher, Adam. "Raw Oysters Really Are Aphrodisiacs Say Scientists (and Now Is the Time to Eat Them)." *The Telegraph,* Telegraph Media Group, 20 Mar. 2005, www.telegraph.co.uk/news/uknews/1486054/Raw-oysters-really-are-aphrodisiacs-say-scientists-and-now-is-the-time-to-eat-them.html.

Kennedy, Victor S., et al. *The Eastern Oyster: Crassostrea Virginica*. Maryland Sea Grant College, 1996.

Kent, Bretton W. *Making Dead Oysters Talk: Techniques for Analyzing Oysters from Archaeological Sites*. Published by Maryland Historical & Cultural Publications for Maryland Historical Trust, Historic St. Marys City, Jefferson Patterson Park and Museum, 1992.

King, Ledyard. "Florida, Georgia Flush out Arguments before Supreme Court in 'Water Wars' Case." *USA Today*, Gannett Satellite Information Network, 9 Jan. 2018, www.usatoday.com/story/news/politics/2018/01/08/florida-georgia-flush-out-arguments-before-supreme-court-water-wars-case/1013651001/.

Kristeva, J. *Powers of Horror* (1980) (trans: Roudiez, L.). New York: 1982. Columbia University Press.

Kurlansky, Mark. *The Big Oyster: New York on the Half Shell*. New York: Ballantine Books, 2006.

Lipinski, Jed. "Shucker for a Day: Oysters, Immigrants and an Aching Back." *NOLA.com*, NOLA.com, 5 May 2016, www.nola.com/business/2016/05/h-2b_immigration_oyster_proces.html.

Manganiello, Christopher J., *Southern Water, Southern Power: How the Politics of Cheap Energy and Water Scarcity Shaped a Region*. U. North Carolina Press, 2017.

McCay, Bonnie J. *Oyster Wars and the Public Trust: Property, Law, and Ecology in New Jersey History*. University of Arizona Press, 1998.

McMurray, Patrick. *Consider the Oyster: A Shucker's Field Guide*. New York, Thomas Dunne Books: 2007.

Miller-Medzon, Karyn, and Robin Young. "Apalachicola Oyster Industry Struggling To Recover After Hurricane Michael." *WBUR*, WBUR, 25 Oct. 2018, www.wbur.org/hereandnow/2018/10/25/apalachicola-oyster-industry-hurricane-michael.

Morris, John C. *The Case for Grassroots Collaboration: Social Capital and Ecosystem Restoration at the Local Level*. Lexington Books, 2013.

"The Oyster Guide." *The Oyster Guide RSS*, www.oysterguide.com/maps/gulf-coast/.

The Oyster's My World, theoystersmyworld.com/tag/dyets-dry-dinner/.

Petrolia, Daniel R. "Hurricanes and Water Wars Threaten the Gulf Coast's New High-End Oyster Industry." *Salon*, Salon.com, 9 Nov. 2018, www.salon.com/2018/11/11/hurricanes-and-water-wars-threaten-the-gulf-coasts-new-high-end-oyster-industry_partner/.

Pittman, Craig. "Supreme Court Finally Rules on Florida's 30-Year Water War with Georgia. And It's Not over." *Tampa Bay, Florida News*, 28 June 2018, www.tampabay.com/news/environment/Supreme-Court-finally-rules-on-Florida-s-30-year-water-war-with-Georgia-And-it-s-not-over-_169506140.

Philpots, John R. *Oysters and All about Them*. Richardson, 1891.

Portman, Jed. "Why We Love Apalachicola Oysters—Garden & Gun." *Garden & Gun*, 19 May 2017, gardenandgun.com/articles/why-we-love-apalachicola-oysters/.

Probyn, Elspeth. *Eating the Ocean*. Duke University Press, 2016

"Protecting Wild Rivers." *American Rivers*, www.americanrivers.org/threats-solutions/protecting-rivers/.

Spear, Kevin. "Apalachicola River Named Most Endangered in Nation." *OrlandoSentinel.com*, 12 Apr. 2016, www.orlandosentinel.com/news/environment/os-apalachicola-most-endangered-20160412-story.html.

Spengler, Teo. "Facts About Oysters in the Gulf of Mexico." *USA Today*, Gannett Satellite Information Network, 15 Jan. 2019, traveltips.usatoday.com/oysters-gulf-mexico-1393.html.

Stott, Rebecca. *Oyster*. Reaktion Books, 2004.

"Study Shows Toxic Effects of Oil Dispersant on Oysters Following Deepwater Horizon Spill." *ScienceDaily*, ScienceDaily, 13 Sept. 2018, www.sciencedaily.com/releases/2018/09/180913160039.htm.

"Tri-State Water Wars (AL, GA, FL)." *Southern Environmental Law Center*, www.southernenvironment. org/cases-and-projects/tri-state-water-wars-al-ga-fl.

Walsh, Robb. *Sex, Death and Oysters*. Berkeley, Counterpoint, 2009.

Waters, Sarah. *Tipping the Velvet*. Virago Press, 2018.

Weiss, Allen S. *Feast and Folly Cuisine, Intoxication, and the Poetics of the Sublime*. State University of New York Press, 2002.

Wennersten, John R. *The Oyster Wars of Chesapeake Bay*. Eastern Branch Press, 2007.

ACKNOWLEDGMENTS

I have so much thank to spread. thank you to oysters and the gulf of mexico. the Apalachicola river. that small swamp behind my father's house. thank you to my mother for support and oyster stew. thank you Catherine Hofmann for your love, patience, and for listening to me read this very long poem aloud on multiple occasions. thank you to my soulmates Coco Wilder, Emerson Rhudy, Karina Soni, Nicole Campbell, Omololu Babatunde, Zaina Alsous. many thanks to my dear friend Sylvia Herbold for lending her artwork to this chapbook. thank you to Laura Jaramillo for all of her kind words. thank you to my teachers Brian Teare, Jena Osman, Gabrielle Calvocoressi, and the long line of patience that preceded them. thank you to my stepdad Vinny for helping me wash and ship shells. thank you to Amy Correia for all the years of friendship filled with road trips to Apalach. for the edits and the encouragement, I'd like to thank my beloved workshop comrades jasper avery, Sean Collins, Royce Drake, Lucas Lozada, Tiana Wilson, Joohyun Kim, Robert Carey, Alex Pulliam, Zan de Parry. I am incredibly grateful for the new and old friendships that sustain me : Autumn Casey, Anne Symons, Darragh Nolan, Evana Roman, Kirsten Lee, Michaela Burney. thank you to my housemates for all the food and kitchen talk : Connie Yu, Devan Spear, Heidi Ratanavanich, M Slater, and Zoe Blickenderfer. and finally, a big thank you to Ander, New Michigan Press, and *DIAGRAM* for giving this poem a body.

BLANCHE BROWN grew up in the Florida panhandle, adjuncts at Temple University, operates a crisis hotline, and collaborates with arts and community-based organizations in Philadelphia. Her writing has appeared in *West Branch*, *Scalawag*, *Indy Weekly*, *Welter*, and elsewhere. She believes oysters offer blueprints for how to reimagine and transform the social.

❁

COLOPHON

Text is set in a digital version of Jenson, designed by Robert Slimbach in 1996, and based on the work of punchcutter, printer, and publisher Nicolas Jenson. The titles here are in Futura.

NEW MICHIGAN PRESS, based in Tucson, Ari`zona, prints poetry and prose chapbooks, especially work that transcends traditional genre. Together with DIAGRAM, NMP sponsors a yearly chapbook competition.

DIAGRAM, a journal of text, art, and schematic, is published bimonthly at THEDIAGRAM.COM. Periodic print anthologies are available from the New Michigan Press at NEWMICHIGANPRESS.COM.

CPSIA information can be obtained
at www.ICGtesting.com
Printed in the USA
BVHW050315270120
570501BV00005B/8